Effective Communication in the Workplace

Learn How to Communicate Effectively and Avoid Common Barriers to Effective Communication

by Anthony Gutierez

Table of Contents

Introduction

Among the crucial ingredients to a business's success is effective workplace communication. It is, therefore, unfortunate that effective communication does not happen smoothly in many companies. This is due to a number of reasons. When managers or supervisors use unclear and vague language, workers are unable to meet their boss's expectations. The situation isn't really helped with today's modern means of communication, such as emails, texts and chats. There is less face-to-face interaction, words are abbreviated and, oftentimes, the message's meaning is lost in these rather impersonal ways of communicating.

It should also be taken into consideration that words are only a small percentage of face-to-face communication. There is tone of voice, body language, and even the words left unsaid that comprise the total meaning of a message. When people talk face-to-face, there is always room for misinterpretation, especially when one only focuses on the words being said and doesn't consider the tone or body language of the speaker. So you can see that it's really much worse in emails, chats, telegrams or text messages. The receiver of the message cannot see the face and body language, and cannot hear the tone of the sender of the message, so the chances of misinterpretation are increased.

Other causes of miscommunication in the workplace include the management speaking only from their point of view and not considering the employee's perspective. For effective communication to occur in the workplace, management and workers must have equal opportunities to voice their concerns. A dialogue should never be one-sided, because that's often a source from which communication problems arise. The fast pace at which the business moves is another element that causes communication problems in a company. In this case, communication is often hurried and leaves a lot of opportunities for the message to be misunderstood.

Ineffective communication in the workplace is one of the leading reasons why many businesses lose profits and valuable resources, such as excellent employees and clients. Companies can miss important opportunities to grow and expand their business when there is poor communication in the workplace. How many good employees – valuable assets to the company – have resigned due to miscommunication, and how many potential clients have been lost due to the inability to deliver the right message? Effective communication must be practiced by all workers, whether managers, supervisors, or those in entry-level positions, to make sure that the daily operations of the company run smoothly.

Whether a business is big or small, management must invest time and money to develop, practice and improve communication skills. People often take effective communication in the workplace for granted, but wiser entrepreneurs recognize that there is a great benefit and much power in the ability to communicate effectively inside the workplace. Messages are clearer and productivity is higher when there is no miscommunication between the employer and the employee, between the workers, and between the people in management positions.

This book is designed to enlighten business owners, managers, supervisors, and employees about the barriers of effective communication in the workplace, what causes them, and how they can be overcome. Read this book and learn how to effectively deliver your message to your boss, workers, or colleagues for greater productivity, cooperation, and understanding.

6

Chapter 1: What is Effective Workplace Communication?

Perhaps one of the reasons that effective communication in the workplace is being taken for granted in some workplaces is because some people don't really know what it means. What is effective workplace communication, anyway?

Today, advanced technology has made it possible for communication in the office to be done without the need for face-to-face communication. Bosses just send emails to the managers and the managers do the same to the supervisors. The supervisors then just relay important updates to the employees through text messages, Skype chat or some other form of digital communication. In the past, when there was important news to be shared with the workers of a company, the upper management would call for a meeting with the middle management and the middle management would have a meeting with the workers afterward. These days, however, there just isn't time to hold traditional meetings. The speed at which businesses move prevents people from connecting on a personal level, and people have learned to sacrifice face-to-face communication for faster business transactions. Meetings are done through Skype chats and people no longer need to travel or be physically present for a conference. And while modern means of communication have their own merits, the quality of communication in the workplace may be suffering. Because of the lack of opportunities to connect on a personal level, communication barriers arise, causing communication problems between the employer and employees, and also between the workers themselves.

In order to have effective workplace communication, people should be able to connect on a personal level. There should be opportunities for face-to-face interaction so that communication barriers can be minimized or removed. When people don't communicate face-to-face, they cannot observe the facial expression, voice, pitch and body language of the people with whom they are communicating. This may lead to misinterpretations on the part of the receiver of the message. Face-to-face communication gives people a chance to clarify the message's meaning. And, although it takes more time than just sending a digital message, face-to-face communication is really more effective than electronic messages.

However, effective communication in the workplace is not limited only to the means by which messages are sent. There are other factors that should also be considered in order to ensure that communication in the workplace is effective. For instance, managers, supervisors and people in middle management positions must also possess good communication skills. They should be courteous when talking with other employees because, when it comes to courtesy in a workplace, position should not be an issue at all. All people in the company, whether boss or employee, must make an effort to speak and behave in a polite or courteous manner when communicating with each other.

All communications must be clear and concise, so as to minimize any chance for misunderstandings. Words must be chosen carefully when relaying important messages and, in case there are misunderstandings, there should always be an opportunity for clarifications. Jargon should not be used when communicating with people outside one's own department because that will only alienate other workers and cause communication barriers. Studies also prove that men and women in the workplace communicate differently. Men, in general, will use less words and gestures than women when communicating. People in the workplace must also be sensitive to race and culture in order to have a more effective communication in the workplace.

Chapter 2: Why Do We Need Effective Communication in the Workplace?

Many modern companies today allot a great deal of time and money to training their workers in communication. It is their goal to have a workforce that is able to communicate effectively. Undeniably, communication skills are essential and very significant to the company's progress. Effective communication helps employers and employees communicate better with each other and with their clients, suppliers and partners in business.

These days, more and more business owners are beginning to understand the benefits of having good verbal and non-verbal communication skills. Many of their employees have conversations with existing clients and potential customers. Employees are required to submit written reports, as well as send emails. It is, therefore, important that employees be able to communicate effectively so that business can flow smoothly. It helps to have a workforce that is able to communicate effectively. Employees that have good communication skills become assets for the company, as they facilitate smooth business transactions. Customers love it when the people they talk to in a company can listen to what they are saying and understand what they need. At the same time, if all people in the workplace practice effective communication, then every worker can connect with each other with minimal or no problems at all.

When there is effective workplace communication, barriers in communication can be reduced or eliminated. A diverse workplace benefits a great deal from effective communication. In most cases, language and cultural differences can create barriers between workers, but this can be reduced when employers and employees alike possess good communication skills. Confusion that can be caused by differences in culture and language can be thwarted with training on diversity and communication. Through effective communication, errors are decreased, misunderstandings are reduced, operations run smoother and productivity is improved.

Effective workplace communication becomes more and more important with the increase of global business transactions. Many companies deal with international clients or have a partnership with companies in foreign countries. They might also have branches in other parts of the world, and having the ability to communicate with people from other cultures can be very beneficial for every business. For instance, American customs can be very different from those in Asian and Middle Eastern countries. It is, therefore, advantageous to have some background about the cultural differences but, most importantly, it's necessary to be able to communicate despite these differences. Those companies that have invested in communication training for their workers will have an easier and more pleasant experience of engaging in global trading. Companies that are looking to expand their business in other countries will greatly benefit from putting their employees in training that can improve their communication skills.

It is not uncommon to hear employees complain about their managers or supervisors due to communication issues. However, with effective workplace communication, managers can create teams that are highly efficient. It's easy for workers to trust each other and their superiors when they practice effective communication. Problems within teams or departments can be reduced and, without unnecessary communication snags, employees can focus on working harmoniously alongside each other. Effective communication allows employees to become more productive, responsible and secure in their roles on the team. Managers with good communication skills can direct their subordinates without creating a hostile work environment. Effective workplace communication brings about positive working environments and relationships between the employees which result in a more productive business. Finally, effective communication boosts morale, and employees that are happy with their jobs will give better work performances.

Chapter 3: What Barriers Prohibit Effective Workplace Communication?

While effective communication in a workplace is essential, there are factors that prevent employers and employees from its benefits. For example, the bigger the company, the more complex communication issues will be. However, let me point out that the basic principles of communication are applicable to all businesses, whether large or small. Among the most common communication problems in companies are the use of wrong communication methods, misunderstandings and failure to confirm whether the message was received and understood.

People who work in upper and middle management must check the level of awareness, understanding and concern among their subordinates before communicating messages. Employees don't know or need to know all things happening in the company. However, there are issues about which they need to be informed, mainly because it concerns them. Companies should also check the level of understanding of its workers about any issues concerning the company, ensuring that any gaps are bridged with effective communication right away.

Modern technology has allowed people to communicate faster, but not necessarily more efficiently. Businesses today benefit a great deal from various methods of communication. The problem lies in choosing and using the appropriate channels for the messages. Companies must know which communication channels are best for the type of message, their target audience and the situation. Some messages can be relayed best through a face-to-face meeting, while some are most effectively disseminated through an email, a chat message or an SMS. It will also greatly depend on the importance of the message to be relayed. The more important the message is, the more important it is to have a face-to-face meeting. One good example is the firing of an employee. A manager will need to schedule a face-to-face meeting with the employee that he or she needs to fire. With a message as important and as sensitive as this, managers should never use any kind of electronic message. Another potential pitfall with communication channels is the possibility that the message may not reach the target audience. For example, a school has chosen to post its graduation announcements and updates through its Twitter and Facebook accounts; unfortunately, not all the school's students have Twitter or Facebook accounts. Moreover, not all of those that have accounts in these social networking sites regularly check their Facebook and Twitter pages. The communication channels used by the school are not effective or useful for all students. On the other hand, if the school limited all its information dissemination to its bulletin boards, the students would need to go to the school grounds daily to check for new updates. Companies should put effort into determining the most appropriate communication channels in order to relay messages more efficiently.

Once the message has been sent, is that really enough? Managers and supervisors must make sure that not only has the message reached the target audience, it must be clearly understood by them. Failure to check for understanding is a common mistake by people who relay messages, and the outcome can be as disastrous as not receiving the message at all. For effective communication to occur there must be two-way communication. This allows the receiver of the message to clarify the message. If he or she has misunderstood, there is a chance for the message sender to explain further and, if necessary, to provide more details to be better understood.

There are also physical barriers to effective workplace communication. Many modern work stations have eliminated cubicles that separate workers. Instead, there is an open space that allows people to communicate more freely. However, recent studies have shown that open offices have reduced productivity, as employees are unhappy about the lack of privacy, noise, opportunities for gossiping and inability to concentrate on their daily tasks. Other barriers to effective workplace communication can include differences in personality. For instance, shy, introverted people tend not to speak with anyone unnecessarily, but keep to themselves and just be a loner. Low self-esteem can also prevent people from communicating effectively to their co-workers. People's differences may prevent effective workplace communication, but good companies can have all kinds of training made available to their employees in order to help them become more effective communicators. Company owners and leaders that understand the power of effective communication know that a workforce with the ability to effectively communicate can bring more business for the company.

Chapter 4: Developing Effective Workplace Communication Skills in 5 Steps

Communication has three main styles – verbal, non-verbal and written. All of these are needed in running a business. Some employees may be good in verbal communication, but have problems effectively communicating through emails and letters. Others can be excellent in verbal and written communication, but may have trouble ensuring that their body language matches their words. Companies need to train their employees so that they can master all three styles of communication. Fortunately, barriers in communication can be eliminated and, with time and practice, all people can communicate effectively. Here are some useful tips on how to improve one's communication skills:

Step 1

Improve your verbal communication style. Always use words that are easy to understand. If you had to choose between using a difficult vocabulary and an easy one, always choose the easy word. That way, you are sure that your listener will understand. Relaying important messages is not the time to impress people with your high knowledge of vocabulary. Remember that your goal is to deliver to your co-workers important information and that you should help them understand it. Don't confuse your target audience by making your words and sentences more complex than they should be. In fact, you should be simplifying your message to reduce any chances of misinterpretation. Speak clearly and use concise sentences to deliver your message.

Step 2

If you are sending a written message, make sure that you read aloud what you have written. Read it at least three times before sending it to the recipients. Many people who are great public speakers have some difficulty when it comes to written communication. Writing is very different from speaking, and written communication is a skill that should also be mastered. It is quite necessary in business communication. Some CEO's even have staff members to write letters and messages for them. So if you are given the task of communicating with your boss, colleague, subordinate or workmates, never take it for granted. Write a draft and, just like in verbal communication, always choose clear, concise words to deliver your message. You actually have an advantage in written communication because, unlike verbal communication, you can check for errors and edit your message until you are satisfied.

Step 3

Body language comprises a huge part of overall communication. Oftentimes, the words we say do not go along with our body language. For example, we say that something is okay, but our crossed arms and unsmiling face says otherwise. Managers and supervisors should learn how to practice open body language when delivering messages to their subordinates. This is done by taking a non-aggressive stance, such as putting both arms at the side of the body, avoiding abrupt gestures and adapting a relaxed posture and a friendly facial expression. Open body language works well for all employees. It creates a non-threatening atmosphere when communicating. Also, always face the person you are talking to and make sure that you have good eye contact. Avoiding eye contact, not facing the person you're talking to, fidgeting and other questionable body language gives the audience the wrong impression, which could affect the meaning of the message. On the other hand, appropriate body language shows sincerity, interest and integrity.

Step 4

Perfect the art of listening. Many individuals have no trouble winning the hearts and minds of people around them by just showing their ability to really listen. Communicating is not only about speaking and delivering your message. It is also about receiving what the other party has to share. That way, there is two-way communication and the conversation is made whole. There are times when employees need to talk about their concerns and voice their issues. Workers, managers and bosses need to practice listening to each other in order to help the company run smoothly. Problems arise when one fails to listen to the other.

Step 5

Attend lectures and take courses to better your communication skills. Who says you've learned all that you need to know? People and situations change every day and we should learn to adapt to all of these changes. There are always new ways and methods to communicate more effectively. Keep abreast of the changes and developments, and learn as much as you can about being able to communicate more effectively.

People can have good communication skills. Even the shyest and most inarticulate person can become a good communicator with time and effort. Effective communication skills allow workers to have better work experiences, and the company benefits greatly from having employees that know how to communicate effectively.

Chapter 5: Workplace Communication Techniques

Through certain communication techniques, effective workplace communication can be attained. Communication skills are very important and business owners are aware that it is necessary for their business to progress. Employers and employees need to interact with each other on a daily basis, and the ability to communicate well cannot be overemphasized. Effective communication in the workplace helps people create good professional relationships. When people in a company have good communication skills, the needs of the company and the workers are fully met. Here are some communication techniques that one can try in order to communicate more effectively:

Step 1

Define your objective. What is your purpose for communicating? Do you need to sell something, influence or persuade your listener, or do you just need to inform? If you determine the purpose of your communication and have a clear goal in mind, then you can communicate to your audience more effectively.

Step 2

Know your audience. You have a certain advantage when you understand your audience. For example, if you are aware of cultural differences between Americans and Asians, then you can find ways to communicate better to your Asian co-workers. At the same time, if you know that your boss has certain preferences and dislikes, you can use this knowledge in your communication. Knowing what your customers need allows you to communicate more effectively and provide better service.

Step 3

Choose the best communication channels. The communication channel that you use should be the best for your audience, not for you. For instance, it is more convenient for you to just text updates to your subordinates. You know that they will have questions, but you still choose this method instead of calling for a face-to-face meeting. Communication channels should also fit your purpose.

Step 4

Prepare your key points. It will be easier for you to deliver your message if you have an outline and categorize it from the most important to the least important points. In addition, your listeners can better absorb the information you are sharing when it is organized. Whether you have to communicate with a group or just one-on-one, it helps to organize your main points. This also eliminates the possibility for speakers to talk endlessly in a directionless manner.

Step 5

Ask if your audience understood your message. After delivering your message, always make it a point to know whether the audience understood what you said. Provide more explanation and information if you were not clear. Check for any misinterpretations and be sure to correct any errors. Repeat the message if necessary. Communication is not effective if nobody understands you, so make sure that your message is clear and understood.

Through these simple communication techniques, you can become a more effective communicator. Effective communication in the workplace can be achieved and everyone can have a more satisfying working experience when there are fewer misunderstandings and fewer problems caused by poor communication.

Conclusion

Effective communication is essential in any workplace. When a company has people that practice effective communication skills, working relationships are better and productivity is higher. Employees tend to respect leaders that can communicate well with their subordinates, and people in middle management appreciate subordinates than can effectively communicate their concerns.

With the existence of effective communication in the workplace, hostile working environments are avoided. Colleagues gain respect for each other, and interactions with bosses, subordinates or colleagues become pleasant and enjoyable. This contributes to the happiness of employees with their jobs and the company that they work for. Believe it or not, employees tend to value their happiness in the workplace more than their salary because, although money is important for all employees, happiness in their jobs and workplaces is deemed more essential.

With globalization, businesses need to invest in improving their communication skills. Effective communication goes beyond public speaking. It is the ability to reach the target audience, to make an impact and to make a connection. Most companies aim to expand their market internationally, and there is a serious need to possess good communication skills. All entrepreneurs should learn how to communicate effectively in order to facilitate better business transactions. However, it is also important that all company employees develop good communication skills. Companies should provide training and lectures for their workers in order to improve their ability to communicate. This is probably the best investment that business owners can make because their employees are at the front lines of their business. They interact with each other every day and are in charge of the business' daily operation. It helps that workers have good working relationships with each other. More importantly, employees interact with present customers and potential clients, so it is imperative that they possess good communication skills.

Diversity is another reason companies need to have effective communication in the workplace. Companies today are growing more and more diverse as time passes. Bosses, managers and workers need to be aware of language and cultural differences among their colleagues. In doing so, communication problems can be avoided and employee dissatisfaction can be decreased or prevented.

In every business, the employee-employer relationship is very important. Employers that show an effort to improve their communication skills and help their employees to do the same are the ones that form long-lasting professional relationships. Moreover, companies that practice effective communication are the ones that can form lucrative business relations.

Finally, I'd like to thank you for purchasing this book! If you enjoyed it or found it helpful, I'd greatly appreciate it if you'd take a moment to leave a review on Amazon. Thank you!

www.ingramcontent.com/pod-product-compliance
Lightning Source LLC
Chambersburg PA
CBHW061236180526
45170CB00003B/1318